Sushi

Sushi

Hideo Dekura

Published in 2014 by
New Holland Publishers
London • Sydney • Cape Town • Auckland

The Chandlery Unit 114 50 Westminster Bridge Road London SE1 7QY UK
1/66 Gibbes Street Chatswood NSW 2067 Australia
Wembley Square First Floor Solan Road Gardens Cape Town 8001 South Africa
218 Lake Road Northcote Auckland New Zealand

www.newhollandpublishers.com

A catalogue record of this book is available at the British Library
and the National Library of Australia.

ISBN: 9781742575308

Managing Director: Fiona Schultz
Publisher: Fiona Schultz
Design: Lorena Susak
Production Director: Olga Dementiev
Printer: Toppan Leefung Printing Ltd (China)

10 9 8 7 6 5 4 3 2 1

Follow New Holland Publishers on
Facebook: www.facebook.com/NewHollandPublishers

Contents

Basics

Introduction

So, what is sushi? Often, we think of sushi as those little rolls of rice wrapped in a piece of dark-greenish, paper-like seaweed, with some tasty fillings such as fish, chicken or vegetables. Sometimes we have seen rice on the outside of those rolls too. And maybe you have even seen different size rolls—big ones and small. If you have been lucky, you may have had sushi from a large sushi platter including decorated sushi, or even pink rice. Maybe you've seen lots of sushi travel past you on a sushi train and it's been hard to choose what to eat—they look so yummy you want to have them all!

The term 'sushi' covers many different kinds of rice and vinegar food, of all shapes and sizes. Some are wrapped in different ingredients, some are not wrapped at all. Each style of sushi has its own Japanese name and these names describe the sushi by its size, shape and ingredients. 'Zushi' is exactly the same as 'sushi' but when used in a compound word, it is always pronounced zushi, for example 'chirashi-zushi'.

A description of the main types of sushi follows. They are all made with rice that is flavoured with vinegar and usually a little sugar and salt. Traditionally, a small amount of wasabi paste was included in the rolls, but these days, in Western countries, wasabi is often served as an optional extra to be mixed in with some soy sauce as an accompaniment. Some sushi are made to size, others are made larger, usually because of the size of the nori sheets, then cut to size later.

Type of Sushi

NORI-MAKI OR MAKI-ZUSHI

Rice rolled in a sheet of dried seaweed, with a filling of various vegetables, egg, seafood or chicken. 'Nori' is the name of the dried seaweed sheet and 'maki' means 'roll'. Nori-maki have different names according to the fillings and their size and shape: hoso-maki are thin, chu-maki are medium-sized and futo-maki are thick rolls.

URAMAKI

Also called California roll or inside-out roll, as it has a layer of rice on the outside. It always has avocado in the filling, which was not common in Japan years ago.

TAZUNA-ZUSHI (ROPE/RAINBOW SUSHI)

Sushi rice rolled with portions of various ingredients, such as smoked salmon, salad leaves or omelette and placed at an angle so that when it is rolled it looks like a rope.

NIGIRI-ZUSHI

A moulded pad of rice topped with seafood. 'Nigiri' means 'pressed in the hand', which is how the sushi is formed. There are different names depending on the type of seafood used. This sushi is not wrapped in nori.

GUNKAN, BATTLESHIP SUSHI

Gunkan is a variation of nigiri-zushi. It is an oval-shaped ball of sushi rice wrapped with nori, with some tasty topping, in a shape that more or less resembles a battleship.

INARI-ZUSHI

A pocket of deep-fried tofu skin called abura-age, stuffed with rice. Inari is the name of the Fox God (known as Kitsune) of rice, agriculture and fertility. It is believed that the Fox God likes to eat abura-age, which is the colour of fox's fur.

TEMARI-ZUSHI (BALL SUSHI)

Temari is a traditional Japanese decorative ball, a bit smaller than a golf ball. As sushi, temari-zushi are round balls of rice with a decorative topping.

CHIRASHI-ZUSHI (SCATTERED SUSHI)

Chirashi-zushi is a great one-dish sushi meal that is easy to prepare at home. Chirashi means 'scattered', and this is what you do: fill a bowl with sushi rice and then scatter the ingredients such as prawns, chopped omelette, tuna, white fish, shiitake mushrooms and sesame seeds decoratively over the rice. Alternatively the ingredients can be mixed with the sushi rice. It is served at room temperature.

OSHI-ZUSHI (PRESSED SUSHI)

Sushi rice pressed into a box mould with other ingredients as a topping or filling. The mould is removed and the rice is then cut into bite-sized pieces. Use cookie cutters as a mould, if you like. Sometimes the moulded form is wrapped with persimmon or bamboo leaves.

FUKUSA-ZUSHI

'Fukusa' is a cloth for wrapping. As sushi, a thin egg crêpe is wrapped around rice and tied up with a string made of vegetable, such as kampyo (dried gourd strip), chives or scallions (spring onions).

SAIKU-ZUSHI AND MATSURI-ZUSHI (DECORATIVE SUSHI)

This type of sushi is a decorative sushi for special events and festivals. The top of nigiri-zushi or maki-zushi are decorated with a variety of colourful and artistic motifs such as flowers or animals, using the usual sushi toppings but presented in unusual ways.

TEMAKI-ZUSHI (HAND-WRAPPED SUSHI)

These are do-it-yourself hand-wrapped cones of nori filled with sushi rice and a variety of ingredients. You can also use other wrap ingredients such as omelettes or rice paper. They make excellent party food. Simply prepare the rice and fillings ahead of time and arrange them attractively in separate bowls or on one large platter. Provide guidance on how to make the rolls.

Equipment and tools

You may never have seen some of this traditional equipment before since which is used when preparing sushi so I have included alternatives you may have in your own kitchen.

HANGIRI (RICE-COOLING TUB)

This is a wide, flat-based wooden tub with low sides, generally made of cypress. It is designed specifically for cooling sushi rice to give the rice the ideal texture and gloss required for Japanese sushi. If you are using a hangiri, wash it well after use, dry it carefully, then wrap it in a cloth and store it face down in a cool, dry place. For a substitute, you may use a wide, wooden bowl.

HASHI (CHOPSTICKS)

There are varieties of hashi, depending on usage, such as wari-bashi (disposable half-split chopsticks) and sai-bashi (long cooking chopsticks) (hashi is pronounced 'bashi' when used in compound words).

In Japan each family member usually has their own pair of chopsticks, which may have attractive colours and designs.

Traditional Japanese chopsticks have thin pointed ends and come in a range of sizes and shapes, with very small ones for children and long ones for larger men, plus extra long ones for cooking. The ideal chopstick measurement is said to be one and a half times the length from the tip of the thumb to the tip of the index finger when the hand is opened to a right angle (90 degrees).

Used to eat and to cook. They should always be set to point to the diner's left side at the table. For formal dining, there is a chopstick rest underneath them. Some people make a chopstick rest out of the paper case when using disposable chopsticks.

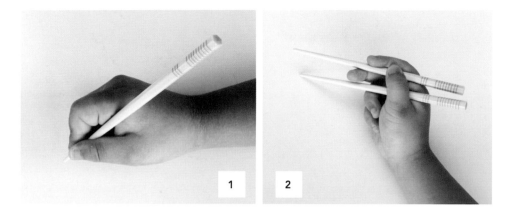

1   2

HOW TO HOLD CHOPSTICKS

- Hold a chopstick as if holding a pen (see photo, left).
- Insert another chopstick between the index finger and middle finger from the base of thumb.
- Line up the points. Grip the lower chopstick firmly at the base of thumb, supported by the first knuckle joint of the ring finger.
- Move the upper chopstick using thumb and index finger. Try to move only the upper chopstick, not the lower one. Try to touch the point of the upper chopstick to that of the lower one.

HOCHO (KNIFE)

Unlike Western knives, which have a double blade, Japanese knives have a cutting blade on one side only, and a wooden handle. The cutting blade is usually on the right side for right-hand users, but left-hand blades can be ordered.

Traditional Japanese knives need extra care to prevent them from rusting. Nowadays, the most commonly used ones are made from stainless steel, which does not rust.

In this book, only basic slicing skills are needed so a kitchen knife will be suitable, as long as it is sharp.

MAKISU OR MAKI-SUDARE (SUSHI MAT)

Makisu is a small mat made of narrow strips of bamboo and it is vital for rolling sushi. Several sizes of makisu are available—some that are wider than a whole nori sheet to much smaller ones. The regular size is about 9½ x 8⅓ in (24 x 21 cm). After using the mat, scrape off any rice with a brush or sponge and dry well. As a substitute, you could use a silicon mat, which is commonly used for dough-making.

MANAITA (CHOPPING BOARD)

Use a chopping board that is wide enough to cut on and not too small. When using a chopping board, place a damp cloth or stopper sheet underneath, to keep it steady. After you've finished chopping, wash the board well and stand to dry properly.

RICE COOKER

You can cook rice in a pot, but using a rice cooker makes it easier to cook rice without any problems or fuss. However, read the booklet before using and always wipe the bowl with a dry cloth when placing the bowl in the rice cooker. I prefer using a rice cooker, which seals tightly when closed.

SHAMOJI (SPOON)

Shamoji is a spoon to fold or scoop rice. It is made from wood (mostly bamboo) or plastic. Before using it, dampen it in water to prevent rice from sticking all over it. For a substitute, you may use a wooden spatula or a flat spoon.

TAMAGOYAKI-KI (JAPANESE OMELETTE PAN)

A Japanese omelette pan is not round, but rectangular-shaped and about 1¼ in (3 cm) deep.

TWEEZERS

TUsed for removing fish bones, Japanese tweezers have wide, flat tips designed to efficiently remove fish bones but you can ask your fishmonger to remove the bones for you.

VEGETABLE PEELER

The Japanese peeler is similar to a potato peeler, but the blade is set at a right angle to the handle, which makes it easy to slice vegetables in thin, long strips. These strips are used for making wrapper-type sushi.

OTHER UTENSILS

- Cooking scissors: used for cutting nori, trimming leaves, etc
- Kitchen scales and measuring cups and spoons
- Bowls
- Saucepans
- Slicer: to use for slicing vegetables
- Spatula: instead of shamoji (a rice spoon) a spatula is used for folding rice or mixing sushi rice
- Strainer: to strain rice, etc
- Vegetable or cookie cutter: to cut vegetables, etc
- Moulds: to prepare moulded sushi with other ingredients. Also small cake tins (pans) could be used as moulds
- Uchiwa (hand fan): These plastic fans are used to cool down rice when preparing sushi rice
- Deep-fryer

Essential ingredients for sushi

KOME (RICE)

Rice (flavoured with a little rice vinegar, sugar and salt) is the basic ingredient for sushi. There are many different varieties of rice. They all look slightly different when they are raw but, most importantly, when they are cooked they have different flavours and other characteristics too. For sushi, the best type is medium or short-grain Japonica rice. It has a good flavour, and it is more glutinous than other types, which means that when it's cooked, it will retain more moisture and be a bit more sticky, so that it clumps together lightly. This is ideal for making sushi, so that the sushi doesn't fall to pieces when we are eating it. Once you have learned how to make sushi with short-grained rice, you may like to experiment with other varieties such as wild rice, black or brown rice (genmai). I have included some recipes to inspire you.

In Japan, people can be very particular about the brand of rice they buy for sushi, but in any country there are always good brands, whether they are imported from Japan or locally grown. Rice should be stored in an airtight container in a dry, cool, dark place. Brown rice will not last as long as white rice because it has a higher oil content.

Remember, when rice is cooked it expands about two and a half times its original volume, so you always end up with more than you started with.

SU (VINEGAR)

When making sushi it is important to add a small amount of vinegar to the cooked rice while it is still hot. Often this is rice vinegar. There is also pre-made sushi vinegar/ seasoning called *awase-zu* (pronounced: ah–wah–se–zoo). It is slightly sweeter than regular rice vinegar. It is mostly sold as a liquid, but is also available in powder form.

COOKING RICE

Ingredients

4 cups short grain rice
4 cups water
extra water

Utensils

rice cooker (highly recommended), rice measuring cup (the measuring cup with the rice cooker is usually smaller than 9fl oz (250ml)), strainer, bowl (a little bigger than strainer), dry towel

USING A RICE COOKER

When using a rice cooker, use the measuring cup provided. Rice should be rinsed well before cooking.

- Using the measuring cup provided with rice cooker, place 4 cups of rice into a bowl that holds twice the volume of rice.
- Pour water into bowl until it just covers the rice. Holding the bowl with one hand, stir rice briskly for 10–15 seconds with the other hand (see photo 1).
- Carefully tip the milky water out, covering rice with one hand (see photo 2).
- At the second and third rinse, add ample water and stir again for about 30 seconds to remove excess starch. Tip out water.
- Run cold water over rice for about 1–2 minutes, until water becomes clear.
- Transfer rice to a fine-mesh sieve to drain and leave for 30 minutes (see photo 3).
- Place rice and measured water into the rice cooker pan (see photo 4). Wipe the underneath of the pan with a dry towel and set it into the rice cooker. Switch on.
- When cooked, leave for 20 minutes to steam.
- Before serving, turn rice over gently with a moistened rice paddle to allow excess moisture to escape as steam.

When rinsing, do not soak the rice for any length of time, as water will be absorbed. When you have left-over rice, keep it in the freezer, wrapped with plastic wrap or in an airtight container. Sandwich bags with a zipper are quite convenient.

USING A SAUCEPAN
Use a stainless steel or non-stick saucepan that has a close-fitting lid.

Ingredients
2 cups (14 oz/400 g) short-grain rice
2 cups (16 fl oz/500 ml) water

- Rinse the rice 3 times to remove the excess starch as for the rice cooker method.
- Soak the rice in water for 30 minutes. Drain the rice and transfer it to a saucepan.
- Add the cold water.
- Bring the water to the boil over high heat, then put on the lid and turn the heat to the lowest setting. Cook for 12 minutes, turn off the heat and allow to steam for another 10 minutes with the lid on. Carefully remove the lid after 10 minutes. The hot rice is now ready for the next stage of mixing.

COOKING BROWN RICE

Ingredients
3 cups (1 lb 5 oz/600 g) brown rice
3½ cups (1 pint 9 fl oz/870 ml) water

Utensils
rice cooker (highly recommended), rice measuring cup, strainer, bowl

Brown rice does not need rinsing as much as short grain rice. However, pick it over to remove small foreign substances such as grit or twigs.

USING A SAUCEPAN

- When cooking brown rice in a saucepan, you need to cook it for about 40 minutes over low heat without scorching.

USING A RICE COOKER

- Place a strainer over a bowl just a little bigger than the strainer.
- Add rice.
- Add water until it just covers the rice.
- Hold the strainer with one hand and briskly stir the rice for 10–15 seconds with the other hand.
- Lift the strainer, drain off and discard the murky water.
- After draining, add more water to cover the rice and allow it to soak for at least 1 hour or overnight.
- Drain rice well and transfer it to the rice cooker.
- Add the water to the rice cooker pan.
- Wipe the base of the pan with a dry towel and set it in the rice cooker.
- Close lid, turn on and allow to cook.
- When the rice cooker has turned off, leave for 20 minutes to steam.
- The hot rice is now ready for the next stage of mixing.

COOKING COLOURED RICE

Ingredients
3 cups (1 lb 5 oz/600 g) short-grain rice
1–2 tablespoons wild rice

- Cook coloured rice using the same method as Cooking Rice.

MAKING SUSHI RICE

Ingredients

2½ fl oz (75 ml) rice vinegar
1¾ oz (50 g) superfine (caster) sugar
pinch of salt
3 cups (1 lb 6 oz/600 g) hot cooked short-grain rice (see recipe for Cooking Rice)

> NOTE: Pre-made sushi vinegar (*awase-zu*) is also available, either liquid or powder.

Utensils

measuring cup, rice paddle, dry towel or mitten, hangiri (as a substitute for hangiri, a wooden salad bowl is ideal), hand fan, rice paddle or a wooden spatula, muslin cloth or kitchen towel

- To make sushi vinaigrette, mix the rice vinegar, sugar and salt in a cup or bowl, until sugar has dissolved (see photo 1).
- Moisten the wooden bowl with a damp towel.
- Using a damp rice paddle, transfer the hot cooked rice into the bowl and spread evenly in the base
- Gradually pour the vinaigrette over the rice (see photo).
- Mix the rice evenly around the bowl with a slicing action (see photo 3).
- While mixing, cool the rice with a hand fan so that the rice absorbs the vinegar mixture and becomes glossy (see photo 4).
- Cover with a muslin cloth and let it cool down until slightly warm.

Making pink sushi rice colouring

Makes about 3 tablespoons

Ingredients
2 oz (60 g) red beetroot
2½ fl oz (75 ml) rice vinegar
2¼ oz (70 g) superfine (caster) sugar
pinch of salt

Utensils
cheese grater (shredder) with a tray, bowls, strainer

- Rinse the raw beetroot and grate (shred) using a cheese grater into a bowl (see photo 1).
- Add the vinegar, sugar and salt and mix well (see photo 2).
- Strain into another bowl (see photo 3).

Note: You can freeze any leftover liquid in cubes if you do not use it all.
You can make beetroot jam (see recipe) with the beetroot pulp and use the jam as sushi decoration, sauce or topping.

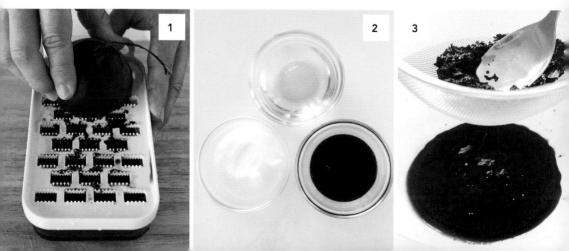

MAKING PINK SUSHI RICE

Makes 2 cups (11 oz/300 g) cooked pink sushi rice

Ingredients
1 lb 2 oz (500 g) cooked sushi rice (see recipe)
1¾–2¼ oz (50–70 g) pink sushi rice colouring (see recipe)

Utensils
bowl, rice paddle

- Place the sushi rice in a bowl and drizzle pink sushi rice mixture over the rice (see photo 1).
- Mix everything together with a moist rice paddle, until the rice is evenly coloured (see photos 2 and 3).

Making beetroot jam

Ingredients

1 teaspoon mirin
2 tablespoons water
¼ cup (1¾ oz/55 g) superfine (caster) sugar
2 oz (60 g) beetroot pulp (leftover from Pink Sushi Rice Colouring recipe)

Utensils

saucepan, wooden spoon

The strained leftover beetroot pulp can be used as topping on sushi, as a decoration and also as a taste enhancer. Mirin is only used for cooking but it does contain alcohol. It will keep for 1 week in the refrigerator.

- Place all the ingredients in a saucepan and set over moderate heat. Bring to the boil and reduce until it becomes thick like jam, about 5 minutes, stirring constantly with a wooden spoon (see photo 1 and 2).
- Leave to cool to room temperature and use for toppings (see photo 3).

Japanese Groceries

ABURA-AGE (THINLY SLICED, DEEP-FRIED TOFU)

Abura-age are thin, slightly sweet, flavoured sheets of deep-fried tofu, which are made into little pouches. These pouches are filled with sushi rice to make inari-zushi. They are usually bought already flavoured from the freezer section in Japanese grocery shops, but if you buy them unflavoured you can prepare them yourself. You can also cut them into strips and add them to miso soup.

AONORI (GREEN NORI POWDER)

This coarsely ground nori can be used to sprinkle onto inside-outside sushi rolls and is also used as a coating for tempura.

DASHI (JAPANESE STOCK)

Instead of chicken or beef stock, the Japanese use dashi, which is their own version of stock. It is also available in powdered form from Asian grocers and some supermarkets.

DENBU (LIGHTLY MINCED FISH)

A pink mixture made from white fish and natural colouring, used in chirashi-zushi or as a decoration for sushi rolls or nigiri. It is sometimes called sakura-denbu (cherry denbu) and is sold in small packs.

FURIKAKE (SPRINKLE-SEASONING)

Furikake is a dried condiment that is sprinkled over dishes, especially plain cooked rice. It typically consists of a mixture of some of the following: sesame seeds, ground fish, shredded nori, egg, katsuo-bushi or vegetables. Yukari is a type of furikake made from seasoned dried red shiso. Furikake is used as a decoration for sushi, especially inside-out rolls.

GARI (PICKLED GINGER)

Gari are ginger slices that have been pickled in salt and sweet vinegar. They are a delicate pink colour and are available in bottles or vacuum-packs. Small amounts of gari are eaten between bites of sushi to freshen the mouth, and tastes quite tangy.

Sometimes bright-red, vinegared ginger, is available, called beni-shoga. It is not used with sushi, but sometimes with chirashi-zushi (scattered sushi).

1

2

3

4

Making gari

Makes 7 oz (200 g)

Ingredients
3½ fl oz (100 ml) rice vinegar
1½ oz (40 g) superfine (caster) sugar (if you like sweeter gari, add extra sugar)
pinch of salt
7 oz (200 g) fresh, young ginger (young ginger is a slightly pinkish, creamy colour and only available in season from early summer)

Utensils
saucepan, wooden spoon, peeler or slicer (or knife), a container with a lid

- Combine the vinegar, sugar and salt in a pan and stir it over a low heat until the sugar is dissolved. Allow to cool.
- Using a vegetable peeler or slicer, peel the skin from the ginger and then slice the ginger into paper-thin slices. Soak them in cold water for 15 minutes. Rinse and drain well.
- To reduce the bitterness, pour boiling water over the ginger, then drain and squeeze when cool enough to handle.
- Pickle in the sweet vinegar mixture overnight in the refrigerator in a non-metallic bowl. Transfer the ginger slices to a container with an airtight lid.

Making a gari rose as a garnish

- Arrange 5–6 pieces of gari across a clean chopping board, each one slightly overlapping the piece next to it.
- Pick up the edge nearest you and roll to the other end.
- Stand the roll on its end and slightly open the top out so it resembles a rose. Serve as a garnish.

GOMA (SESAME SEEDS)

Black and cream/white sesame seeds are commonly found. You can buy them roasted or toast them in a dry frying pan over medium heat. Move them around in the pan with a wooden spoon so that they turn golden brown but do not allow them to burn. Roasted sesame has a stronger aroma and a darker colour. For sushi, sesame seeds are often used as a final decoration for coating or topping.

KAMABOKO (FISH CAKES)

These Japanese-style fish cakes are available frozen. There are various forms, some of them dyed pink. Kamaboko can be used in chirashi-zushi.

KAMPYO (DRIED GOURD SHAVINGS)

Sliced and dried gourd is used in ribbon-like strips. Before being used in sushi, kampyo is tenderised and seasoned. You can buy it already cooked, but the dried variety is more common in Asian grocery shops.

PREPARING KAMPYO FOR SUSHI

Ingredients

²/₃ oz (20 g) dried kampyo
1 cup (8 fl oz/250 ml) dashi stock
2 tablespoons superfine (caster) sugar
1½ tablespoons soy sauce

Utensils

bowl, saucepan, strainer, wooden spoon

- Put some water and a pinch of salt in a bowl and rub the kampyo in the bowl with your hands until it softens. Rinse under running water.
- Put water in a pan and bring it to the boil. Add the kampyo and cook for 10 minutes.

- Drain and transfer to a bowl of cold water and drain again.
- Put dashi and sugar in a pan and bring it to the boil. Add kampyo to the dashi and cook over low heat for 5 minutes. Add soy sauce and simmer for about 3 minutes.
- Cool ito room temperature.

KANI-KAMA
An artificial crab-meat stick made of fish paste and other ingredients. It is used as a filling for nori rolls.

KATSUO-BUSHI (BONITO FLAKES)
Katsuo-bushi is used to make stock for miso soup. It is also used in the preparation of some sushi ingredients such as abura-age for inari-zushi. It is also used as a topping for salads. It is sold in a packet (see Miso Soup recipe).

MIRIN (COOKING RICE WINE)
Mirin is a type of sweet sake used in cooking to enrich the flavour of a dish or to glaze the surface of the food that is being grilled (broiled). It contains alcohol but this will evaporate when heated.

MISO (FERMENTED SOYBEAN PASTE)
Miso is a tasty ingredient made from fermented soybeans, malt and salt. There are several varieties of miso, which may be distinguished by colour, ingredients and method or area of production. It is used as a basic ingredient in soups, for flavouring in stews and sauces.

NORI (SHEETS OF SEAWEED)
Used for making sushi rolls. The sheets measure 7½ x 7¾ in (19 x 20 cm) and are sold in a packet. Once the wrapping has been opened, use the nori as soon as possible, or keep it in a closed plastic bag in the refrigerator. Make sure you buy pre-roasted nori, known as yaki-nori, not the raw type. Nori are smooth on one side, rough on the other. The smooth side goes on the outside of the roll. Nori sheets have a slight linear

pattern. This should be aligned with the stitching on the bamboo mat when using the whole nori sheet to make large rolls.

PANKO
Panko is a variety of Japanese breadcrumbs. It is crispier than Western breadcrumbs and is often used on fish or seafood.

SHIITAKE (SHIITAKE MUSHROOMS)
Fresh or dried shiitake mushrooms are available. Dried shiitake are mainly used to make stock. For sushi, sliced shiitake cooked with soy sauce and sugar are used for rolls or chirashi-zushi.

SHOYU (SOY SAUCE)
Shoyu is the most common accompaniment with sushi. It is a fermented sauce made from soy beans, wheat, salt and water. It can be used as a versatile seasoning, in cooking or as a base for soup. There are various types of soy sauce, depending on ingredients and character. For sushi, choose naturally brewed, not chemically made soy sauce, such as Kikkoman brand soy sauce. Organic soy sauce, low/less-salt soy sauce, tamari soy sauce or gluten-free soy sauce is also suitable.

TAKUWAN (PICKLED DAIKON)
Pickled white radish, also known as daikon, is called *takuwan*. There are several varieties and colours of *takuwan*, but the most common one used for sushi rolls is yellow *takuwan*. It is sold whole or halved in a packet.

TOBIKO (FLYING FISH ROE)
See Fish section.

TOFU (SOYBEAN CURD)

A white curd of custard-like texture made from soy beans, which can be added to miso soup. For soup, use the Japanese 'silken' variety. Tofu must be kept in the refrigerator, in water deep enough to cover it. Once opened, change the water at least twice a day. Stored this way, tofu will last a couple of days, but it is best used straight after opening.

UMEBOSHI (PICKLED DRIED UME-PLUMS)

The Japanese plums, *ume-boshi*, can be large or small, hard or soft. After being dried, they are usually pickled with salt and coloured red by being preserved with red shiso leaves. They are sold in a packet, either with pits or pitted, or even as a paste in a tube or bottle.

The large ones can be used for sushi rolls when the seed is removed. The taste may be very salty and tangy, though less salty, somewhat sweeter ones are also now available. They are good when combined with other ingredients and are used in dressings and sauces as well.

WAKAME (WAKAME-SEAWEED)

Wakame is a type of seaweed available in dried form and often used in miso soup. Dried wakame must be soaked before using.

WASABI (JAPANESE GREEN HORSERADISH)

A native Japanese plant that is found growing near clear spring water. Fresh wasabi has a lovely texture, distinctive pungent tang and aroma. However, fresh wasabi is expensive and largely unavailable outside Japan, so powdered wasabi, which is mixed with a small amount of tepid water to make a paste, is more common. In Japan, a small amount of wasabi is usually included in the sushi. When it is served separately, it can be mixed with a little soy sauce.

OTHER INGREDIENTS

Other than Japanese groceries, you can use these general ingredients for sushi: ham, cheese, chicken, smoked salmon, eggs, mayonnaise—try whatever you like!

Vegetables

Fresh vegetables are great fillings for sushi and for making decorations when you serve the sushi. Vegetables are eaten raw or blanched, or sometimes cooked with extra flavouring, such as soy sauce.

- asparagus spears
- avocado
- bell peppers (capsicums)
- carrots
- sweet corn kernels
- cucumber (Lebanese cucumber is suitable)
- English spinach, fresh or blanched
- green beans/French beans
- green salad leaves
- lettuce

- lotus root (renkon), cooked
- mizuna leaves
- okra
- red radish
- scallions (spring onions)
- snow peas (mange tout and snow pea sprouts
- tomato
- watercress
- white daikon (white radish)

Try some of these vegetables in your sushi:

Herbs

Shiso (Japanese basil)

Shiso is a Japanese summer herb with a pleasant aroma. It is used raw, not only sliced finely with food, but also decoratively as a whole leaf. There are two types, the green and the red, but the green shiso is most commonly used. Dried shiso is called yukari and is available as a sushi sprinkle topping.

Sometimes shiso plants are sold at nurseries. It can be grown easily at home in the garden or in planters. You can also buy shiso from Japanese groceries during summer.

These non-Japanese herbs are also used in sushi:
- cilantro (coriander)
- mint

Fish and seafood

You may be able to purchase a packet of salmon, king-fish or tuna block that is of sashimi quality (that is raw fish), pre-cut for sushi, which is very convenient. These fish are suitable for sushi:

BURI (KING FISH)
This is a long, slender fish covered with tiny round scales. The back is dark green and the belly part is silvery white. In the centre there is a yellow line, which runs the length of the body. They come as big as 33 lb (15 kg), but you can buy sashimi-quality filleted kingfish.

MAGURO (TUNA)
Tuna is one of the most popular fish for sushi because of its rich red colour and full-bodied flavour. Purchase only a block the size you need, and check that the flesh is firm.

SALMON
The orange colour of salmon is very attractive on a plate. If salmon is unavailable, substitute ocean trout. Smoked salmon is handy too for using in sushi-rolls or chirashi-zushi (scattered sushi). Salmon caviar is expensive but small amounts can be used as a garnish for nigiri-zushi (hand-moulded sushi), chirashi-zushi (scattered sushi) or gunkan (battleship sushi).

UNAGI (EEL)
Filleting eel is quite difficult even for adults so it is better to purchase flavoured grilled (broiled) eel in an airtight plastic pack from the freezer section of Japanese grocery shops. Always follow the directions on the packet.

Eel is used for nigiri-zushi, chirashi-zushi and nori-rolls.

OTHER SEAFOOD
Caviar (salmon roe)
Used for decoration or gunkan (battleship sushi).

Ebi (jumbo shrimp/king prawns)
This is one of the most popular seafoods for sushi.

Ika (squid)
If using raw squid, they should be sashimi quality. Ika is often used for nigiri-zushi.

Tobiko (flying fish roe)
Tobiko is used for decoration, especially for inside-out rolls. Orange-coloured tobiko is common, but green and golden ones are also available.

Other products
Canned tuna, canned salmon, canned crabmeat, crabmeat stick.

Slicing fish fillets

To slice fish for sushi topping, it is best to start with a rectangular block of fish about 2¼ in (6 cm) across and 1½ in (4 cm) high. Of course, the block you have purchased will not be cut to these measurements, so it will need to be cut. A large fish, such as tuna, may be easy to cut. With other fish, such as salmon, try to cut the fish into a block, although the ends and sides may not be very even. With salmon or white fish, you can often cut following the existing angle of the fillet.

First slice off a triangular piece to make an angled edge to work with (any scraps can be used in rolled sushi).

With your knife on a slant to match the angle of the working edge of the block, cut slices about ⅛ in (3–4 mm) thick. The last piece of the block will also be triangular.

The method is also used with smaller filleted fish, adjusting the knife angle to suit the fillet. With fish such as tuna the resulting slices will be uniform and rectangular. With smaller fillets, you may have triangular edges or thinner slices. Sometimes you may need to use more than one slice for a piece of nigiri-zushi.

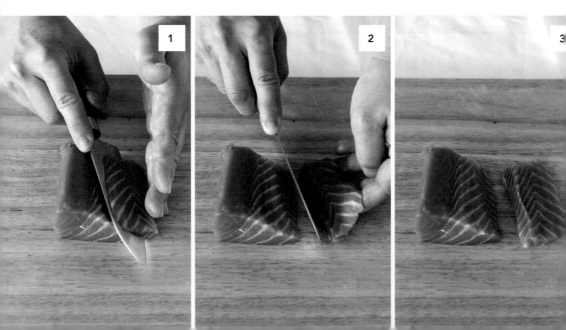

Preparing jumbo shrimp (king prawns) for sushi toppings

Ingredients

6 jumbo shrimp (king prawns)
pinch of salt
½ cup (4 fl oz/120 ml) rice vinegar
¼ cup (2 fl oz/60 ml) water
1 tablespoon superfine (caster) sugar

Utensils

bamboo skewers, saucepan, chopping board, small knife, tray or bowl

- In salt water (about 36fl oz/1 litre and a pinch of salt), Rinse the raw seafood in a bowl containing 1¾ pints/ 1 litre of salted water then wipe with kitchen paper.
- To keep the shrimp from curling during parboiling, pierce with skewers along the belly side from head to tail (see photo 1).
- Bring some water to the boil in a saucepan and add a pinch of salt. Simmer the shrimp for 3 minutes over moderate heat, then plunge into a bowl of cold water. Remove the skewers. Remove the shells, but leave tails intact. Devein (remove the vein running along the back) using a small knife (see photo 2).
- Place the shrimp on a chopping board and, with a small knife, make a slit on the belly side to open up like a butterfly then gently flatten out.
- Combine the inegar, water and sugar in a tray or bowl and place the shrimp in this mixture until ready to use (see photo 3).

Garnishes and decorations

SHREDDED NORI

Used for topping such as chirashi-zushi (scattered sushi). Fold up a sheet of nori and cut it into long thin slices.

PLASTIC FISH SOY BOTTLES

For picnics or in a lunch box, these disposable small bottles are useful. You can purchase them from Japanese grocery shops. You can keep the bottles when you purchase takeaway sushi as they can easily be refilled. Firstly, put some soy sauce into a small bowl. Insert the top opening part of the bottle into the soy sauce, squeeze out the air, and release your finger pressure to suck up the fluid.

EGG MIMOSA

It is used for decoration on sushi or flower-shaped carved vegetables.

EGG MIMOSA

Makes 1 tablespoon egg mimosa

1 egg

- Place an egg gently in a saucepan of water.
- Bring it to the boil and cook until hard-boiled, about 15 minutes.
- Allow the egg to cool. Remove the shell and egg white and take out the egg yolk. Place the yolk into a fine strainer and, using a spoon, sieve the yolk through the strainer into a small container (see photo).

GREEN LEAVES, SUCH AS CAMELLIA LEAF, BAMBOO, HARAN

Camellia leaf, bamboo leaves are used only for garnishing sushi, either to make the dish look pretty or to give the dish some colour when you serve it. Use a knife or cooking scissors to cut out shapes (see photo right).

FLOWER-SHAPED VEGETABLES

Use a vegetable or cookie cutter, to cut sliced vegetables into various shapes.

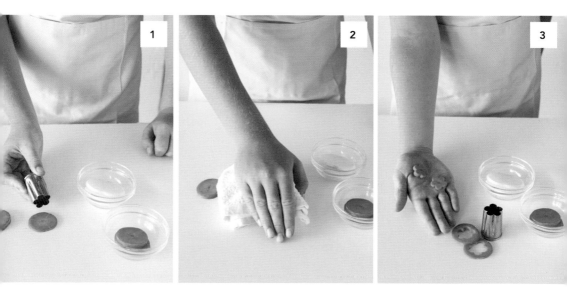

Radishes and cucumbers

Vegetables can be decoratively carved for use as garnishes. When deciding which garnish is best suited for your sushi, consider the colours of the other ingredients. Flowers, leaves and other designs drawn from nature are traditionally used. Remember that these carved vegetables should not be the main element on the plate.

MAKING A RADISH FLOWER

1 red radish

- Slice off the root end of the radish (see photo 1). Make three thin cuts, spacing them evenly around the radish (see photo 2).
- Make three more thin cuts behind each first cut, making sure that the cuts meet near the base of the radish. Do not cut all the way through (see photo 3).
- Holding the base of the radish, gently pull out the centre portion (see photo 4).
- Place egg mimosa (sieved, hard-boiled egg yolk) in the middle of the flower to create the pistil of the flower.

Fillings for nori rolls

When making nori rolls, one or more of the following fillings can be used. The preparation is always the same.

Vegetables

- Lebanese cucumber: cut lengthways, seeded and cut into long thin sticks (see photos opposite).
- Carrot: peeled and cut lengthways into strips and cooked with a small amount of sugar until just tender. Carrots strips may also be used raw.
- Asparagus, French beans, snow peas (mange tout): blanched.
- Avocados: cut lengthways into six equal strips.
- Tomatoes: cut in half, seeded and sliced into thin segments.
- Scallions (spring onions): the bottom portion trimmed and sliced lengthways.
- English spinach: blanched and cooled.
- Green salad leaves: rinsed and drained well.
- Bell peppers (capsicum): red or yellow, core and white veins removed. Cut into narrow strips.

SWEETENED COOKED CARROT

Makes enough for 1 roll of sushi

1 small carrot
1 teaspoon superfine (caster) sugar
½ cup (4 fl oz/120 ml) water

Peel and cut the carrot into lengthways strips and cook in a saucepan with the sugar and water for 5 minutes over a low heat.

Set aside to cool down.

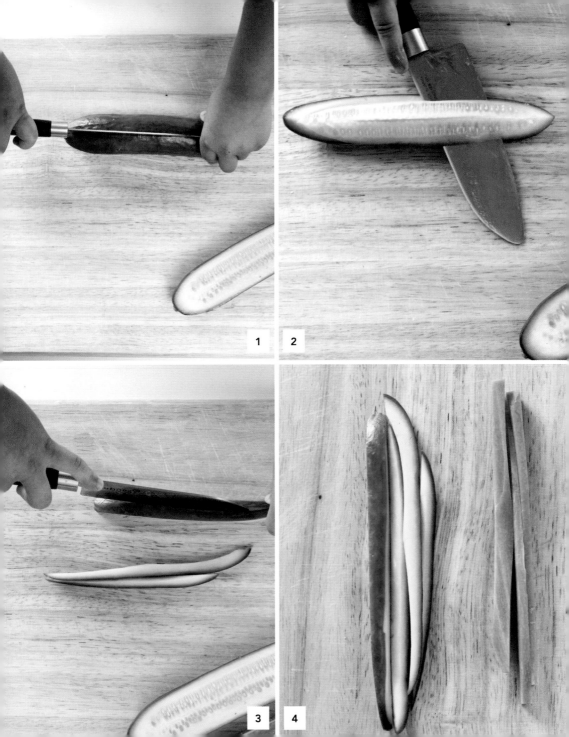

MEAT, EGG AND OTHER FILLINGS

- Egg omelette strips (see Square Omelette recipe)
- Crab meat: sliced, broken into appropriate-sized sticks. Imitation crab meat or seafood sticks may also be used.
- Pickled daikon: cut into sticks.
- Sliced fresh tuna: it should be sashimi-quality and very fresh. Otherwise, it should be cooked.
- Canned tuna: well-drained, mixed with mayonnaise or miso.
- Salmon: fresh, smoked or canned, well drained.
- Jumbo shrimp (king prawns): cooked, or tempura (see Fish and Seafood in Introduction)
- Grilled eel: purchase pre-cooked grilled (broiled) eel and slice it.
- Chicken, teriyaki chicken and deep-fried chicken: cut into strips. Other varieties such as tandoori chicken can also be used (see recipes for Teriyaki Sauce.
- Beef: Thinly sliced beef, available from Asian butchers or grocery shops, braised in teriyaki sauce (see recipe for Teriyaki Sauce).
- Pork: lean pork steaks, sliced and then stir-fried in teriyaki sauce.
- Cheese strips: choose your favourite cheese.
- Ham strips: choose your favourite ham.
- Sausages: choose your favourite sausages and cook, then slice into smaller portions.

PASTE AND SPRINKLES

- Umeboshi (pickled plum) paste
- Sesame seeds
- Furikake

MAKING SOY SAUCE-FLAVOURED CANNED TUNA

These days you can find a huge variety of canned tuna in the shops. You can choose your preferred type, or maybe you'd like to add a little zest with soy sauce.

1 small can tuna* (approximately 3½ oz/100 g) in brine
1 teaspoon soy sauce
1–2 teaspoons superfine (caster) sugar

*Instead of tuna, you could use a can of salmon.

- Lightly squeeze the liquid out of the canned tuna.
- Place tuna, soy sauce and sugar in a saucepan.
- Cook over a low heat for about 5 minutes, stirring constantly. Remove from the heat and allow to cool.

MAKING SALMON FLAKES

pinch of salt
3½ oz (100 g) salmon fillet

- Sprinkle salt over the salmon and leave for 10 minutes.
- Place under the broiler (grill) until cooked on one side. Turn and cook the other side.
- Allow to cool. Using your hands, break up the salmon into flakes.

Making avocado tuna

¼ avocado, peeled and seed removed
1½ oz (40 g) canned tuna
pinch of salt
1 teaspoon white sesame seeds
½ teaspoon lemon juice

- Mix all the ingredients in a bowl with a fork.

Making minced chicken in soy sauce

3½ oz (100 g) minced chicken
1 tablespoon mirin
1 tablespoon soy sauce
1 teaspoon superfine (caster) sugar
1 teaspoon water

- Combine all the ingredients in a saucepan over a low heat.
- Stir with chopsticks until the mince has cooked through and turned brown.

TERIYAKI SAUCE

makes about 1 cup (8 fl oz/250 ml)

Teriyaki sauce is also available from Japanese or Asian groceries or major supermarkets, but you can make your own.

4 tablespoons superfine (caster) sugar or raw sugar
4 tablespoons soy sauce
4 tablespoons mirin
1 teaspoon fresh ginger juice (made by grating fresh ginger
   and squeezing over a bowl), optional

- Combine all the ingredients in a saucepan and bring to the boil. Reduce the heat and simmer for 3 minutes.

TERIYAKI CHICKEN

A few drops of vegetable oil
7 oz (200 g) chicken thigh or breast*
1 cup (8 fl oz/250 ml) teriyaki sauce (see recipe)

- Drop a little oil onto the base of the frying pan and swirl to coat.
- Heat the pan over a medium-high heat and add the chicken.
- Fry over moderate heat until browned on each side.
- Add the teriyaki sauce and cook over low heat until cooked through.
- Once it is cooled down, slice into bite-sized pieces.
- *Beef, salmon or tuna can be used instead of chicken.

SQUARE OMELETTE

makes 3 strips for rolls

3 eggs

pinch of salt

1 teaspoon soy sauce

2 tablespoons dashi

1 teaspoon superfine (caster) sugar

1 tablespoon oil, soaked onto a piece of kitchen paper

- Break the eggs into a bowl and beat with a fork or chopsticks. Add salt, soy sauce, dashi and sugar and stir well.
- Rub the oiled kitchen paper over the surface of the pan and heat up over moderate heat.
- Gently pour in a third of the mixture to cover the base of the omelette pan. Use a spatula to press out any air bubbles. When the omelette sets and becomes dry, run a spatula around it to loosen (see photo 1).
- With spatula or chopsticks, fold one-third of the omelette from far side toward centre, then fold this over onto the remaining portion closest to you (see photo 2).
- Using the oiled kitchen paper, wipe over the empty section of the pan, slide the first omelette portion to the other end of the pan and pour in another third of the mixture, lifting the cooked omelette up to let it flow underneath (see photo 3 and 4).
- When firm, fold the thicker portion over toward you as before, making a thick flat roll (see photo 5).
- Continue adding mixture, cooking until firm and folding to make a triple-layered omelette (see photo 6).
- Remove from the heat. Turn omelette onto a plate to cool it down.
- For nori roll fillings, slice into strips.
- For nigiri-zushi cut into pieces 1in (2.5cm) wide and 2½in (7cm) long.
- The omelette can also be eaten on its own, as tamagoyaki, cut into cubes.

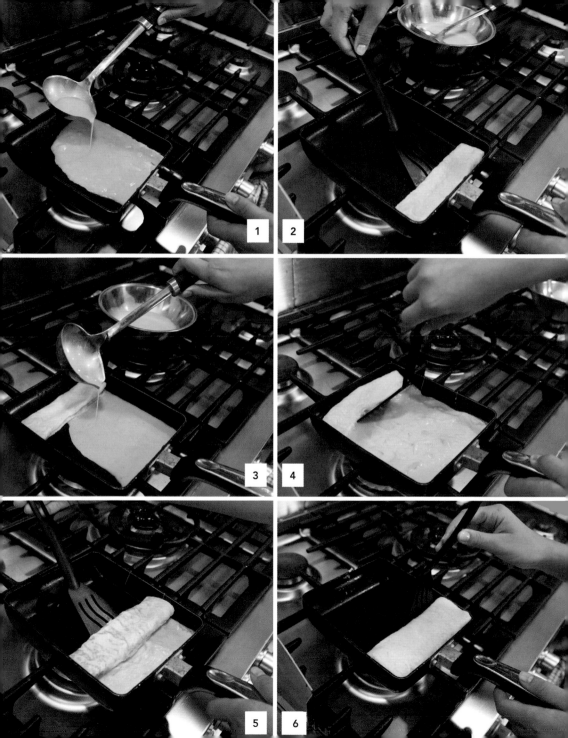

Tandoori Chicken

1 lb 2 oz (500 g) chicken breast fillet

½ teaspoon salt

1 tablespoon curry powder or tandoori paste

1 cup plain (natural) yogurt

½ teaspoon ginger powder or fresh ginger (grated/crushed)

½ teaspoon grated garlic

1 tablespoon tomato paste

- Put the chicken in a bowl. With a fork, spear the chicken and rub it all over with salt.
- Cover the chicken with all the ingredients and rub in with your hands. Refrigerate overnight or for half a day.
- Preheat the oven 400°F (200°C/Gas mark 6). Put the chicken on a baking sheet and remove some of the excess marinade with kitchen paper.
- Bake in the oven for about 10–15 minutes, or until cooked.

Deep-frying

Cooking with oil, especially deep-frying, needs more care than other cooking, as the temperature of oil rises to more than 300°F (150°C).

Safety tips for deep-frying:

- Overheated oil can ignite. If the oil is allowed to become too hot, it will burst into flames. In case of an oil fire, NEVER USE WATER. Cover with a kitchen fire blanket or a lid if possible. Make sure to turn off the heat.
- Oil and water do not mix. When cooking, keep water away from the hot oil. If water drops onto the heated oil, hot oil will splash out. This can cause burns. That is why you need to remove any excess water from foods before frying to prevent the oil from splattering. Letting ingredients sit on paper towels or coating them in flour, batter or breadcrumbs is also effective.
- Preferably use a deep-fryer or a large saucepan or wok.
- Add oil to the cold pan, leaving some space at the top, at least 4 in (10 cm), which allows a safety margin as oil bubbles up.
- Heat the oil over medium heat. If you have a deep-frying thermometer, use it to measure when the oil is 350°F (180°C). If not, drop a few breadcrumbs into the oil, and when they quickly float up, the oil is ready.
- Do not overcrowd in the pan when deep-frying. Leave a bit of space around each of the ingredients to cook evenly.
- When removing food from the oil, always use a pair of tongs or a mesh ladle.

Shrimp (prawn) tempura

4 green jumbo shrimp (king prawns)
1 tablespoon potato starch
tempura batter

> Note: Tempura batter is available from Japanese or Asian grocery shops and should be made according to the instructions on the packet. The batter can also be made by mixing 2 oz (60 g/½ cup) tempura mix flour with ½ cup (4 fl oz/120 ml) refrigerated water. If you are unable to obtain tempura flour, make a batter using ½ cup (2 oz/60 g) all-purpose (plain) flour, ½ beaten egg and ½ cup (2 fl oz/55 ml) cold water.

To prepare the shrimp, first remove the head. Without cutting off the tail, remove the shell (see photo 1).

Use a bamboo stick to remove the vein from the back. Repeat with the other 3 shrimp. Rinse and pat with kitchen paper.

Place the shrimp with its belly facing up on a chopping board. With a small knife, make 4 deep scores to prevent curling. After cutting, bend the shrimp in the opposite direction to its natural curve to further straighten it (see photos 2 and 3).

Pat with kitchen paper to dry. Coat the shrimp with potato starch on a plate.

To make tempura batter, place flour in a bowl. Add refrigerated cold water. Using a fork or pair of chopsticks, roughly combine. Do not mix too much as it will become too starchy – a few lumps in the mixture are ok. Keep the mixture in the refrigerator (see photo 4).

Put the oil in a deep-fryer, pan or wok and heat the oil to 350°F (180°C). To check the temperature, drop a small amount of the tempura batter into the oil, and when it quickly floats up, it is ready.

Shrimp (prawns) in breadcrumbs

4 green jumbo shrimp (king prawns)
2 tablespoons all-purpose (plain) flour
1 cup (3 oz/85 g) panko breadcrumbs or breadcrumbs
1 egg, beaten

Prepare the shrimp according to the shrimp tempura recipe.
   Put the flour on a plate, the beaten egg in a bowl and the breadcrumbs on a plate.
   Holding one shrimp by the tail, coat the shrimp with flour (see photo 1).
   Dip the coated shrimp in the beaten egg (see photo 2).
   Transfer onto the breadcrumbs and coat evenly, pressing firmly with the fingers (see photo 3).
   Repeat with the remaining shrimp.
   Prepare the oil in a deep-frying pan and heat to 350°F (180°C).
   Deep-fry the shrimp until golden brown.
   With tongs or a mesh ladle, transfer onto a rack or kitchen paper, to allow excess oil to drain (see photo 4).

Panko breadcrumbs are available fin larger supermarkets.

1

2

3

4

Tatsuta-age (savoury deep-fried chicken)

7 oz (200 g) chicken thigh or breast
2–3 tablespoons potato starch, for dusting
vegetable oil, for deep-frying

MARINADE
2 tablespoons soy sauce
1 tablespoon honey or sugar
1 teaspoon crushed garlic and 1 teaspoon grated (crushed) ginger, added to the
marinade (optional)

Cut the chicken into cubes, each piece about 1 oz (30–35 g).
   Combine all the marinade ingredients in a cup and stir.
   Place the chicken in a plastic bag.
   Pour the marinade into the bag.
   Close the bag and massage the marinade around the chicken.
   Refrigerate for at least 30 minutes.
   Remove the chicken from the bag and pat with kitchen paper.
   Put potato starch on a plate and coat the chicken.
   Heat the oil to about 350°F (180°C). To check the temperature, drop in a small piece
of bread and if it comes up to the surface quickly, it is ready. Deep-fry the chicken
cubes for 1 minute, take out and set aside for 1 minute on a tray or rack to steam.
   Deep-fry the rested chicken again for two minutes and drain well on a rack or kitchen
paper.

Tonkatsu (Japanese-style fried pork)

1 piece pork loin (approximately 5 oz/150 g)
salt, to taste
black pepper, to taste
1 tablespoon all-purpose (plain) flour
2–3 tablespoons panko breadcrumbs or fine breadcrumbs
1 egg
vegetable oil, for deep-frying

Dust the pork with salt and pepper.

Put the flour and breadcrumbs on separate plates. Break the egg into a bowl and beat it with a fork. Arrange the flour, egg and breadcrumbs in a row.

Transfer the pork onto the flour and coat liberally. Pat off excess flour (see photo 1).

Dip the pork into the egg and coat thoroughly so that the breadcrumbs will stick (see photo 2).

Place pork onto the breadcrumbs and coat on both sides, pressing firmly with your hands (see photo 3).

Heat the oil to about 350°F (180°C).

Deep-fry the pork until golden brown, turning a couple of times. Drain well over a rack or kitchen paper (see photo 4).

Cut to the required size when cool.

For sushi roll, before deep-frying, you can also create pork sticks by cutting the pork loin into strips and coating, then deep-frying.

Dressings

You can use your favourite brands of mayonnaise. Japanese mayonnaise contains more egg yolk than Western varieties and is generally not as sweet.

KIWI FRUIT MAYONNAISE
This is suitable for vegetable rolls.

makes ½ cup (4 fl oz/120 ml)

½ kiwi fruit, flesh scooped out
2 tablespoons mayonnaise

Place all kiwi fruit and mayonnaise in a bowl and mash with a potato masher or fork.

LEMON JELLY

3 tablespoons lemon juice
1 tablespoon superfine (caster) sugar
1 tablespoon water
1 teaspoon gelatine, soaked in 1 teaspoon water
pinch of lemon zest

Combine the lemon juice, sugar and water in a saucepan. Over low heat, bring it to the boil.

Add the gelatine and cook until dissolved, stirring with a spoon. Remove from the heat and transfer into a bowl.

Leave to cool, then refrigerate until set. Break up into small pieces with a fork.

Sweet soy sauce mayonnaise

¼ teaspoon soy sauce
¼ teaspoon raw sugar or superfine (caster) sugar
2 tablespoons Japanese mayonnaise

Put the soy sauce and sugar in a heatproof bowl.
   Heat in a microwave for 5 seconds on high heat. Mix until the sugar is dissolved.
   Once it has cooled down, add the mayonnaise and mix well.

Soy sauce jelly

1 teaspoon gelatine powder
1 teaspoon water
¼ cup (2 fl oz/60 ml) dashi stock
2 tablespoons soy sauce
½ teaspoon superfine (caster) sugar

Soak the gelatine with 1 teaspoon water in a small saucer and leave for 5 minutes.
   Add dashi, soy sauce and gelatine in a small saucepan (see photo 1).
   Over low heat, cook, stirring with a spoon, until dissolved.
   Remove from the heat and transfer the gelatine mixture into a bowl or container.
   Refrigerate until set.
   With a fork, roughly scramble the jelly (see photos 2, 3 and 4).

Wasabi mayonnaise

Wasabi is as hot as English mustard. You can control the heat with the amount of
wasabi powder/paste you use.

2 tablespoons mayonnaise
1 teaspoon wasabi paste or less for a milder taste

Mix all the ingredients in bowl until combined.

Nori-maki

Nori-maki

Nori-maki rolls are the most popular type of sushi. There are many varieties, both thin and thick, ones with nori on the outside or nori on the inside. The thin rolls usually have Japanese names, such as *kappa-maki*, or kampyō-*maki* and the thick ones may have American names, such as California rolls (inside-out rolls), Boston rolls (with grilled [broiled] salmon skin), Philadelphia rolls (with cream cheese), spider rolls (with soft-shelled crab tempura).

Before you start, you need to prepare some sushi rice (see Essential Ingredients for Sushi in Introduction) and fillings (see Basic Techniques).

Things to know before making sushi rolls:
- Place the bamboo sushi mat on a cutting board with the loose strings furthest away from you. If the mat's bamboo sticks are flat on one side, place that side up.
- Arrange the nori, fillings and rice close around the board.
- Make sure you have a bowl of vinegar water, called 'tezu' (1 teaspoon rice vinegar in 1 cup (8 fl oz/250 ml) water) handy, for wetting your hands when you handle the rice.
- Place a sheet of nori on the bamboo mat, smooth side down, so that the length is parallel to the bamboo sticks. Stand in front of the bamboo mat.
- Some people encase their bamboo mats in plastic wrap. This makes it both easier to work with and easier to clean, especially for beginners. I prefer to use a bamboo mat without plastic—I like to feel the natural texture of the mat.

Avocado tuna roll

makes 1 thin roll, 6 pieces

1½ oz (40 g) canned tuna
¼ small avocado
½ teaspoon lemon juice
pinch of salt
½ nori sheet
2½ oz (80 g) sushi rice

Using a fork, mash the tuna and avocado together in a bowl. Add the lemon juice and a pinch of salt and combine.

Place the nori on a sushi mat.

Put sushi rice on the front left corner and with moistened fingers spread the rice over the nori sheet, leaving 1 cm (1/3 in) of bare nori at the far end.

Arrange the avocado and tuna in a line along the centre.

Roll mat over once, away from you, pressing ingredients in to keep roll firm, up to the rice-free part.

With the mat still covering the nori, but not the rice-free portion of nori, hold the rolling mat in position and press all around to make the roll firm using your fingers.

Lift up the top of the mat and roll over a little bit more to seal the joins.

With the mat still in place, roll once more, and use your fingertip pressure to shape the roll in a cylindrical form.

Remove the mat and place the roll on a chopping board and slice.

EBI-ROLL (SHRIMP/PRAWN ROLL)

makes 1 roll, 6 pieces

1 tablespoon mayonnaise
¼ teaspoon curry powder
½ sheet nori
2½ oz (80 g) sushi rice
2 jumbo shrimp (king prawns) tempura
small salad leaves

Mix the mayonnaise and curry powder in a small bowl.

Place the nori on a sushi mat.

Put the sushi rice on the front left corner and with moistened fingers spread the rice over the nori sheet, leaving 1cm ($^1/_3$ in) of bare nori at far end (see photo 1 on the following page).

Spread mayonnaise mixture on top (see photo 2).

Arrange the salad leaves on top of the shrimp (see photo 3).

Arrange the shrimp along the centre with the tails poking out from each end of nori (see photos 4 and 5).

Roll the mat over once, away from you, pressing the ingredients in to keep the roll firm, up to the rice-free part.

With the mat still covering nori, but not the rice free portion of nori, hold rolling mat in position and press all round to make the roll firm with the fingers.

Lift up the top of the mat and roll over a little bit more to seal the joins (see photo 6).

With the mat still in place, roll once more, and use fingertip pressure to shape the roll in cylindrical form.

Remove the mat and place the roll on a chopping board and slice.

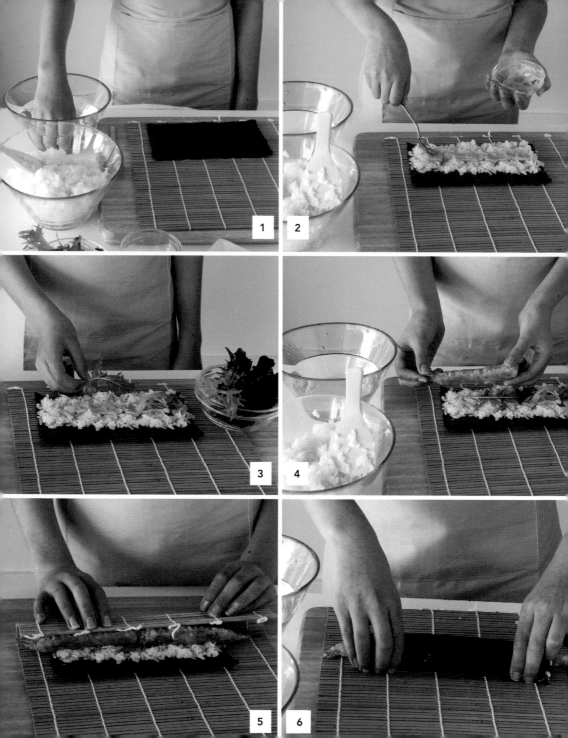

Futo-maki (thick roll)

makes 1 roll, 8 pieces

1 nori sheet
5 oz (150 g) sushi rice
1 teaspoon furikake or tobiko
3–4 fillings of your choice (see Basic Techniques — Preparing fillings for nori rolls)

Place the nori on the sushi mat (see photo 1, following page).

Put the sushi rice on the front left corner, moisten your fingers and spread rice over the nori sheet, leaving ¾ in (2 cm) of bare nori at the far end.

Sprinkle furikake or spoon tobiko along the centre of the rice using the back of a spoon.

Arrange the filling along the centre (see photo 3).

Roll the mat over once, away from you, pressing the ingredients in to keep the roll firm, leaving ¾ in (2 cm) of nori rice-free (see photo 4).

With the mat still covering the roll, but not the rice-free portion of nori, hold the rolling mat in position and press all round to make the roll firm with the fingers (see photo 5).

Lift up the top of the mat and roll over a little bit more to seal the joints.

With the mat still in place, roll once more, and use fingertip pressure to shape the roll in a cylindrical form.

To slice the roll, you will need a chef's knife, chopping board and damp kitchen towel or cloth (see photo 6).

Place the roll on the dry chopping board. Moisten the knife with a damp towel and cut the roll in half, then cut each half in half again. Cut each quarter in half to make 8 equal-sized pieces in total.

Sweet soy sauce-flavoured beef roll

makes 1 roll, 6 pieces

drop of vegetable oil
1 oz (30 g) thinly sliced beef (available from Japanese grocery shops in the frozen
    section, or some Asian butchers)
1 teaspoon superfine (caster) sugar
1 teaspoon soy sauce
few small salad leaves
½ sheet nori
4oz (120g) sushi rice

Put oil in a frying pan and heat it up.

Add the beef, sugar and soy sauce and stir until it is cooked through. Remove from the heat and set aside.

Place nori on sushi mat.

Put sushi rice on the front left corner and with moistened fingers spread rice over nori sheet, leaving ⅓ in (1 cm) of bare nori at far end.

Arrange the beef and salad leaves in a line.

Roll the mat over once, away from you, pressing the ingredients in to keep the roll firm, up to the rice-free part.

With the mat still covering the nori, but not the rice-free portion of nori, hold the rolling mat in position and press all round to make the roll firm with the fingers.

Lift up the top of the mat and roll over a little bit more to seal the joins.

With the mat still in place, roll once more, and use fingertip pressure to shape the roll in cylindrical form.

Remove the mat and place the roll on a chopping board and slice.

CHU-MAKI (MID-SIZE ROLL)

makes 1 roll, 8 pieces

1 nori sheet
4½ oz (130 g) sushi rice
2–3 fillings of your choice (see Basic Techniques – Preparing fillings for nori rolls)

Place whole nori on the sushi mat.

Place rice on the middle of the left-hand side of the nori sheet. Leave rice-free space on both sides.

Moisten fingers in the tezu and spread rice evenly across the nori, leaving ¾ in (2 cm) strips at the front and back.

Place filling on the centre and roll as for a thin roll.

With a moistened knife, slice the roll in half and then into 6–8 pieces.

Uramaki

Uramaki (inside-out/california roll)

makes ½ roll, 4 pieces

Inside-out rolls may look difficult, but they are actually easier to roll for the beginner than ordinary sushi rolls. Plastic wrap (cling film) is used to keep the sushi rice from sticking to the bamboo mat. If the roll is not served straightaway, it can be wrapped in plastic wrap to prevent it drying out. You can enjoy trying many different toppings for the outside of the sushi rice, such as flying fish roe, egg mimosa, furikake (sprinkles), sesame seeds or flaked green nori. You can also make mini inside-out rolls, using a quarter sheet of nori, and 1½ tablespoons rice on a small sushi mat.

½ cup (2½ oz/75 g) sushi rice
½ nori sheet
3–4 fillings of your choice (see Basic Techniques – Preparing fillings for nori rolls)
2 teaspoons sesame seeds on a plate

Place nori sheet on mat (see photo 1 on the following page).
 Put the rice on the front left corner of nori and then spread it out with moistened fingers, covering the entire nori sheet (see photos 2 and 3).
 Cover the sushi rice and mat with a sheet of plastic wrap, folding it over the edges to attach it to the back of the mat, or cut plastic wrap slightly larger than the mat and place over the nori and rice on the mat (see photo 4).
 Insert one hand under the nori and carefully pick up the rice-covered nori by the corners, quickly turn it over and place upside down on the mat (see photos 5 and 6).
 Arrange fillings along the centre of nori (see photo 7) Proceed to roll the rice and nori on the mat, pressing in on the ingredients with your fingertips, stopping ¾ in (2 cm) short of the end (see photo 8).
 Lift up the mat, roll back a little, then roll forward to join the edges. Using gentle pressure, shape into oval or square shapes (see photo 9). Transfer the roll onto a dry board. Cut into four equal-sized pieces. Coat with sesame seeds.

5

6

7

8

TIGER ROLL

1 nori sheet
less than ½ cup (2½ oz/75 g) sushi rice
1 tablespoon tobiko (flying fish roe)
1 tablespoon black roasted sesame seeds
3 fillings of your choice, such as beef teriyaki, green salad, carrot sticks (see Basic
    Techniques – Preparing fillings for nori rolls)

Follow the same method as listed in the recipe for Uramaki, inside-out/California roll.
    After you have made the roll and sliced it, coat half the pieces with tobiko and the
rest with black sesame seeds. Arrange in alternate colours, like tiger stripes, on a plate.

DRAGON ROLL

makes 1 roll, 5–6 pieces

1 cup (2 oz/55 g) sushi rice
2 crab sticks or 4 cooked jumbo shrimps
   (king prawns), peeled
1 Lebanese cucumber
1 packet grilled (broiled) eel, frozen or
   vacuum packed

2 spring onion stems, for whisker
   decoration
2 cherry tomatoes, to garnish

Prepare eel by heating according to instructions on the pack. Allow to cool.

To prepare cucumber: using a peeler, peel cucumber to make about 6 strips.

Place a bamboo mat on a dry area and put the nori on the mat. With moistened fingers, spread rice all over the nori sheet and place eel on the center horizontally.

Place a sheet of plastic wrap on top.

Insert one hand under nori and carefully pick up the rice-covered nori by the corner. Quickly turn it over and place upside down on the mat.

Arrange crab sticks and cucumber along the centre of nori.

Proceed to roll rice and nori on the mat, pressing in on ingredients with your fingertips, stopping ¾ in (2 cm) short of the end.

Lift up mat, roll back a little, then roll forward to join the edges. Use gentle pressure to shape.

Transfer the roll onto a dry board and with a chef's knife, cut each roll in half, then cut both into 3 pieces.

Present them on a plate and decorate using spring onion and tomatoes.

Tazuna-zushi

TAZUNA-ZUSHI (ROPE SUSHI/RAINBOW ROLL)

makes 1 roll

Tazuna means 'twisted rope' so tazuna-zushi is a rope-shaped sushi. Choose three ingredients in different colours for toppings to make it look like a rainbow.

2 cooked jumbo shrimp (king prawns)
1 slice cheese or 2 thin egg omelette
    strips (cut the same size as the
    cucumber strips)

3 strips cucumber (see Basic Techniques
    — preparing fillings for nori rolls)
about 6 oz (175 g) sushi rice
carrot, blanched snow peas (mangetout)
soy sauce, to serve

Peel each shrimp and remove the head and tail. Place on a chopping board. With a sharp knife make a deep slit down the underside of each shrimp and spread open like a butterfly.

With a small knife slice the cheese in half.

Place a chopstick horizontally slightly above the centre, on the plastic wrap placed on the bamboo mat (see photo 1).

Along the chopstick, arrange alternate slices of cucumber, shrimp and cheese, just touching, diagonally across the centre of the plastic wrap (see photo 2).

With moist hands, spread sushi rice evenly over the slices. Take away chopstick (see photo 3).

Hold the edge of the mat and fold in half. Push firmly with your hands to form a neat cylinder (see photos 4 and 5).

Unroll the mat and transfer the sushi to a dry board (see photo 6).

Remove the plastic wrap and cut each sushi roll widthways into half and then halve each piece (see photo 7).

Serve with soy sauce.

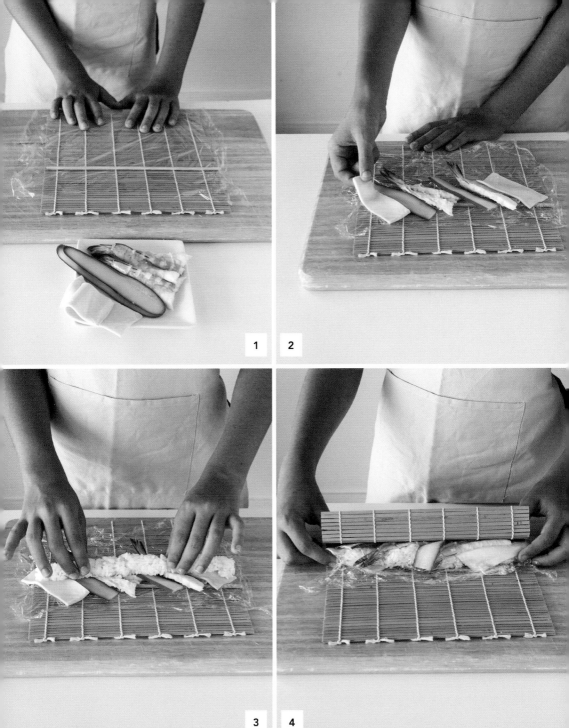

1

2

3

4

Mini tazuna-zushi (mini rope/rainbow roll)

Using the same method as tazuna-zushi, except this is only a quarter of the size.

2½ oz (75 g) sushi rice
2 cucumber strips (2 in/5 cm long)
1 carrot or ham stick
1 strip of cheese or thin egg omelette
soy sauce, to serve

Prepare your ingredients following the method from the tazuna-zushi recipe.
   Place a chopstick horizontally slightly above the centre.
   Along the chopstick, arrange cucumber, carrot or ham, cheese or omelette, just touching the next diagonally across the centre of the plastic wrap.
   With moist hands, spread sushi rice evenly over the slices.
   Hold the edge of the mat and fold in half. Push firmly with your hands to form a neat cylinder.
   Unroll the mat and transfer the sushi to a dry board.
   Remove the plastic wrap (cling film) and cut each sushi roll in half.
   Serve with soy sauce.

Nigiri-zushi

Nigiri-zushi

Nigiri-zushi literally means hand-moulded sushi, which is an oblong-shaped white sushi rice combined with toppings, usually slices of raw fish or other seafood. It looks very simple, but can be difficult to master, particularly with some of the delicate seafood toppings. It might be a good idea to get started with some simple toppings. Variations of nigiri-zushi are gunkan (battleship sushi) and temari-zushi (hand-ball sushi).

GUNKAN (BATTLESHIP SUSHI)

When making gunkan, remember that moistened hands are good for touching the sushi rice, but it is best to have dry hands when handling nori because nori is like paper and will shrivel up when wet. When you are making these sushi, prepare all the rice shapes first, leaving the wrapping until last, otherwise the nori will become wet and may break or go soggy.

Usually, the toppings are loose ingredients and in Japan, the most popular toppings are salmon roe (caviar), flying fish roe (tobikko), and chopped tuna. In this book, we have used canned tuna, corn, shredded steamed chicken and salad leaves, with soy sauce or mayonnaise. Soy sauce jelly, lemon jelly or beetroot jam can also be used for decoration (see Basic Techniques for recipes).

Toppings

- jumbo shrimp (king prawns) (see Fish and Seafood)
- grilled (broiled) eel (see below)
- avocado (see below)
- salmon, fresh or smoked
- snow peas (mangetout), cooked
- egg omelette, sliced
- ham, sliced
- cheese, sliced
- chicken teriyaki (see Teriyaki Chicken recipe), steamed or grilled (broiled) chicken
- beef (see below)
- sausage, grilled and cut in half or sliced
- spam (popular in Hawaii and Korea), sliced and cooked

Nigiri-zushi in gunkan style (battleship)

- caviar
- sea urchin
- canned tuna
- canned salmon
- chicken, grilled (broiled) and shredded
- fruits, such as blueberries

HOW TO PREPARE TOPPINGS

Avocado
Place avocado lengthways on a board.

Hold avocado with one hand and with a medium-sized knife slice slowly cut down the centre lengthways around the pit, starting from the top end.

Hold the avocado and twist clockwise with the hands and rotate to separate the two halves.

Slip a tablespoon in between the pit and fruit and gently remove the seed.

Cut into 4 pieces.

Peel away and discard the outer skin and slice the flesh.

Beef
Use sliced roast beef or thinly sliced beef in teriyaki flavour for your nigiri-zushi.

To make teriyaki beef, marinate 3½ oz (100 g) thinly sliced beef (available from Japanese grocers or Asian butchers) with 1 teaspoon teriyaki sauce (see recipe). Lightly stir fry.

Grilled (broiled) eel
Warm up a pack of eel following the instructions on the packet. Transfer onto the board and slice (see Slicing Fish Fillets recipe).

GUNKAN WITH TERIYAKI CHICKEN AND ALFALFA

makes 4 pieces

1 sheet of nori

2½ oz (80 g) sushi rice, divided into 4 portions

a handful of alfalfa or small salad leaves

1¾ oz (50 g) cooked marinated chicken teriyaki, chopped finely (see Teriyaki Chicken recipe)

Cut the nori about 1x 6 in (2.5 x 15 cm) long with scissors.

Moisten your fingers with tezu, pick up one portion of sushi rice in your hand and gently shape into an oval/rectangular form. Place on a dry plate. Repeat with the remaining rice (see photo 1).

With the rough side of the nori facing the rice, wrap a strip of nori all round the rice and gently press overlapping edges to secure. If they do not stick together, put a couple of grains of crushed rice in between the layers to hold ends together (see photos 2 and 3).

With a spoon or fingers, arrange the alfalfa leaves and chicken on top of the rice inside the ring of nori (see photos 4, 5 and 6).

NIGIRI-ZUSHI

makes 8 pieces

5½ oz (160 g) sushi rice
8 pieces of toppings (select from variety of toppings list)
wasabi, if you like it hot
gari (pickled ginger), for the garnish
soy sauce, to serve

Prepare all of the toppings.

Moisten the hands with the vinegar water and pick up about 1 tablespoonful rice. Form into a ball, pressing gently with the hand but do not squeeze tightly (see photos 1, 2 and 3, on following page).

Place one topping in the palm of your other hand. If you like wasabi, spread on a dab of wasabi with one finger.

Place rice on the topping and with the index and middle fingers press firmly to form a mounded shape (see photo 4).

Roll sushi over and press again with two fingers against the topping (see photo 5 and 6).

Rotate sushi 360 degrees and press again with two fingers against the topping (see photos 7 and 8).

Arrange on a platter. Garnish with pickled ginger and serve with soy sauce.

5

6

7

8

Tomato and avocado nigiri-zushi

½ tomato
½ avocado, de-seeded and sliced
3½ oz (100 g) sushi rice, divided into 5 portions
5 nori strips, about ¾ in (2 cm) wide and 4 in (10 cm) long
mayonnaise or sesame seeds, for decoration

Slice the tomato and avocado to make 5 pieces.

Dampen your fingers with tezu, pick up 1 sushi rice portion in your hand and gently shape into an oval/rectangular form. Place on a dry plate. Repeat with the remaining rice.

Arrange tomato slices on the sushi shape and top with avocado.

Wrap nori band over sushi, encasing tomato and avocado.

Decorate with mayonnaise or sesame seeds if you like.

CUCUMBER NIGIRI-ZUSHI

makes 5 pieces

1 Lebanese cucumber

3½ oz (100 g) sushi rice, divided into 5 portions

5 nori strips, ¾ x 4 in (2 x 10 cm)

3 teaspoons ume-boshi (Japanese salted plum) paste (sold in a tube at Japanese grocery shops)

Place the cucumber on a board and with a peeler, peel 1 strip of outer skin along the length of the cucumber and discard. Using the peeler cut 5 thin strips.

Moisten your fingers with tezu, pick up sushi rice in your hand and gently shape into an oval/rectangular form. Place on a dry plate. Repeat with the remaining rice.

Starting underneath the sushi rice, wrap the cucumber strip over the top, along the length of the rice, leaving the end hanging free, creating a sweeping effect

Wrap a nori strip across the top of the sushi and cucumber, making a band. Seal ends together underneath.

Top with ume-boshi paste on nori as decoration.

CORN MAYONNAISE GUNKAN

makes 4 pieces

1 sheet of nori
1½ oz (40 g) corn kernel, frozen or fresh, cooked and cooled
2 teaspoons mayonnaise
2½ oz (80 g) sushi rice, divided into 4 portions
8 slices cucumber

Cut the nori into strips 1 x 6 in (2.5 x 15 cm) with scissors.

Mix the corn and mayonnaise in a bowl.

Moisten your fingers with tezu, pick up sushi rice in your hand and gently shape into an oval/rectangular form. Place on a dry plate. Repeat with the remaining rice.

With the rough side of the nori facing the rice, wrap the nori all round rice and gently press the overlapping edges to secure.

With a spoon or fingers, arrange the corn on top of the rice inside the ring of nori.

Insert two cucumber slices.

Modern gunkan wrapped with cucumber

makes 4 pieces

1 Lebanese cucumber
2½ oz (75 g) sushi rice, divided into 4 portions
2 small cherry tomatoes, sliced
2 black or green olives, sliced
nchovies, cheese, or any other topping of your choice

Using a vegetable peeler, peel off a wide, lengthways slice of cucumber skin and discard it. Place the cucumber on a chopping board, cut side up, hold firmly, and with the peeler, cut a paper-thin slice about 1 x 4 in (2.5 x 10 cm long. (This strip will have a narrow green outer edge of skin and white flesh in the centre. The skin helps the cucumber to stick to the rice.) Cut halfway into one end of the cucumber slice (see photo 1).

Repeat to make three more slices.

Turn the cucumber slice on its side and slide the other end into the cut half (see photo 2). Repeat with the remaining slices.

Moisten your fingers with tezu, pick up the sushi rice in your hand and gently shape into an oval/rectangular form. Place on a dry plate. Repeat with the remaining rice.

Place the rice balls into the middle of the cucumber (see photo 5).

Top with tomato and olive (see photo 6).

MODERN GUNKAN WRAPPED WITH CARROT

makes 4 pieces

1 large carrot
2½ oz (80 g) sushi rice, divided into 4 portions
2 teaspoons canned tuna (squeeze out the liquid from the tuna)
a few small salad leaves
Soy Sauce Jelly (see recipe)

Using a vegetable peeler, peel the skin from the carrot and discard. Place the carrot on a chopping board, cut side up, hold firmly, and with the peeler, cut a wide, lengthways strip of carrot.

Repeat to make 3 more slices.

Moisten your fingers with tezu, pick up the sushi rice in your hand and gently shape into an oval/rectangular form. Place on a dry plate. Repeat with the remaining rice.

Wrap a carrot strip around the outside of each rice shape, either tucking the outer end over the inner end against the rice, or using a toothpick to secure the ends.

Top with tuna, salad leaves and soy sauce jelly.

Temari-zushi (hand-ball sushi)

Temari-zushi is slightly different from nigiri-zushi because you use plastic wrap to shape the sushi into balls.

makes 5 balls

3½ oz (100 g) sushi rice
toppings of your choice:
  2 jumbo shrimp (king prawns), cooked, peeled, deveined and butterflied
  1 small slice prosciutto or any other ham
  1 small piece of smoked salmon
  1 cheese slice
2 nori strips, for decoration
Parmesan cheese, to garnish
dill, to garnish
1 stalk parsley, to garnish
soy sauce, to serve

Roughly divide the sushi rice into 5.
  Arrange a sheet of plastic wrap (cling film) on a board.
  Place a topping ingredient, such as jumbo shrimp, onto the plastic wrap.
  Take a ball of sushi rice and place it in the middle of the topping.
  Draw the edges of the plastic wrap over the topping and rice and twist it together and shape into a ball.
  Repeat with the other ingredients.
  Just before serving, remove the plastic wrap and decorate with nori strip, Parmesan, dill or parsley.
  Serve with soy sauce.

Temari-zushi with Pickled Vegetables

Serves 4

4 thin slices of peeled daikon, cut across the length
4 thin slices of carrot, cut along the length
8 stems mizuna (Japanese water cress) leaves
Salt, to taste
1 kelp sheet (approximatley 10 cm (4 in) square), sliced into thin strips
1 dry or fresh chilli, de-seeded
4 cups (28 oz/780 g) sushi rice
Cabbage or Chinese cabbage
Cucumber
4 slices yellow pickled daikon (see note)
4 myoga (Japanese ginger) pickles (see note)

To make instant pickles, slice the vegetables, then gently rub in the salt. Add the sliced kelp and chilli and keep in a sealed container for a couple of hours or overnight, depending on the texture you prefer.

To make the sushi, arrange a sheet of plastic wrap on the bench and place the pickles in the centre. Using a moistened spoon, scoop up the sushi rice and place on the top of the pickled vegetables.

Draw the edges of the plastic wrap over the rice and pickle. While twisting together, shape into a ball. Repeat with all the ingredients.

Just before serving, remove the plastic wrap and decorate with nori threads.

Note: Pickles are available from Japanese grocery shops.

Caterpillar roll

makes 7 balls

5 oz (150 g) sushi rice
1 teaspoon yukari (seasoned dried shiso) or other rice sprinkles
12 mint leaves, for the feet
7 cherry tomato halves
2 small circular pieces of nori, for the eyes
2 chives, for the antennae
7 drops of mayonnaise
soy sauce, to serve

Place the sushi rice in a bowl and sprinkle on the yukari. Combine well.
   Roughly divide the sushi rice into 7.
   Arrange a sheet of plastic wrap (cling film) on a board.
   Draw the edges of plastic wrap over the rice, while twisting together and shape into a ball.
   Arrange the mint leaves in pairs, in a line on the plate. Remove the plastic wrap and line up the rice balls to form a caterpillar.
   Place the tomato halves on top of the rice balls, then place a drop of mayonnaise on the top of the tomato.
   At one end, arrange nori to make eyes and chives for antennae, to make a head
   Serve with soy sauce.

Mixed nigiri-zushi

Serves 4

8 green jumbo shrimp (king prawns), sashimi quality
8 large white scallops, sashimi quality
200 g (6½ oz) tuna fillet, sashimi quality
Te-zu (made by combining 1 cup (8 fl oz/250 ml) water with 1 teaspoon rice vinegar)
200 g (7 oz) kingfish fillet, sashimi quality
4 cups (28 oz/780 g) sushi rice
wasabi, to serve
soy sauce, to serve

To prepare the shrimp, remove the heads and shells, but leave the tails intact. Devein the shrimp, then make a slit on the belly side to open up like a butterfly. Gently flatten out.

Cut slices of tuna and kingfish fillet along the grain to make pieces 6 x 2.5 cm (2½ x 1 in) and 3 mm (¹/₆ in) thick.

Moisten your hands with the te-zu and pick up about 1 tablespoon of rice. Form into a rectangular-shaped ball, press gently with the hand but do not squash. Pick up a sushi slice with your other hand and spread on a dab of wasabi with one finger of the hand holding the rice.

Place the rice on the sushi slice and, with the index and middle fingers, press firmly to form a mounded shape. Roll the sushi over and press again with two fingers against the fish. Rotate the sushi 180 degrees and press again with two fingers against the fish. Place on a plate.

Inari-zushi

Inari-zushi

Inari-zushi is a pocket of deep-fried tofu skin called abura-age, stuffed with sushi rice. Inari is the name of the Fox God of rice, agriculture and fertility. It is believed that the Fox God likes to eat abura-age, which is the colour of fox's fur.

The abura-age is deep-fried, thin tofu which can be bought from the freezer section in Japanese or Asian grocery shops. To prepare it for inari-zushi, it needs to be further cooked in a mixture of dashi, sugar, mirin and soy sauce. Sometimes you can buy it already cooked, or it can be cooked at home. This cooking gives it a unique sweet and savoury flavour. Although it is only a thin sheet, after it is cooked, it is possible to gently separate it into 2 layers using your thumbs, to create small pouches. It is either square or oblong, and can be sliced in a number of ways. The abura-age pouches are stuffed with sushi rice and may be sealed up or left open, with some toppings.

Preparation of abura-age for inari-zushi

3 abura-age tofu (not cooked), 2 x 4 in (5 x 10 cm)
1½ cups (13 fl oz/375 ml) dashi stock
3 tablespoons superfine (caster) sugar
2 tablespoons mirin
2 tablespoons soy sauce

With a knife or scissors, cut each piece of rectangular abura-age tofu in half to make 2 squares (see photos 1 and 2).

To remove the excess oil from the abura-age tofu, bring 2 cups (18 fl oz/500 ml) of water to boil in a saucepan. Boil the abura-age in the water for a few minutes. Drain. then place on a chopping board and roll with the cooking chopstick or a rolling pin, to squeeze out the water and unwanted oil (see photos 3 and 4).

Using your thumbs, carefully open the abura-age along the cut edges to make 6 pockets.

Put the dashi into a saucepan and bring it to the boil.

Using tongs or a mesh ladle, add the tofu. Add the sugar, mirin and soy sauce (see photos 5 and 6).

To keep abura-age submerged while cooking, place a sheet of baking paper on top. Bring the mixture to the boil and simmer over low heat for about 10 minutes. Remove from the heat and allow to stand until the liquid is cool (see photos 7 and 8).

Using a spatula, remove the tofu and squeeze to remove excess liquid.

Basic inari-zushi

makes 6 pieces

12 oz (350 g) sushi rice

3 prepared abura-age tofu cut in half to make 6 pouches (see Preparation of abura-age for inari-zushi)

Divide the sushi rice into 6 portions.

With moist hands, lightly form the rice portions into small balls, do not squeeze hard.

Fill tofu loosely with sushi rice. If you fill the pouch too tightly, it may break.

Tuck the top ends of the pouch inside, leaving the rice exposed, or overlap to cover the rice.

Use sushi rice mixed with 1 teaspoon roasted white sesame seeds, if you like.

Log-shaped inari-zushi

12 oz (350 g) sushi rice

3 prepared abura-age tofu pouches (see Preparation of abura-age for inari-zushi), sliced horizontally

20 cooked edamame, without pods (green soy beans, available in frozen section at Japanese groceries)

1 teaspoon yukari (Japanese red basil sprinkles)

Divide the sushi rice into two bowls.

Into one bowl add the edamame and combine with a moistened spoon.

Into the other bowl add the yukari sprinkles and mix with a moistened spoon.

Roughly divide each bowl of sushi rice into 3 portions.

With wet fingers, make each portion into a log shape and place it into the tofu pouch.

Tuck the top ends of the pouch inside.

Place plastic wrap on a dry board and put the inari-zushi in the centre.

Wrap and shape like a log. Repeat with the other pouches.

Leave for 20 minutes to set.

Before serving, cut each in half diagonally.

Hana-inari

1 small Lebanese cucumber

1 small carrot

8 prepared abura-age tofu pouches (see Preparation of abura-age for inari-zushi)

10½ oz (300 g) sushi rice

1½ oz (40 g) gari (pickled ginger)

1 teaspoon egg mimosa (see Garnishes and Decorations)

24 green peas, cooked

24 capers

8 snow pea (mange tout) sprouts or green salad leaves

Place the cucumber on a chopping board and with a vegetable peeler slice lengthways. Prepare 8 long slices.

With a peeler, peel the carrot and as with the cucumber, slice and prepare 8 long slices.

Gently open a tofu pouch.

Dip a tablespoon in water and spoon sushi rice into an inari pouch.

Make small rolls with the cucumber and carrot. Arrange on the top of sushi rice along with gari.

Arrange egg mimosa, green peas and capers on top. Insert snow pea sprouts beside them.

Chirashi-zushi

Chirashi-zushi

Chirashi-zushi is sushi rice and toppings, served in a bowl. It is a dish for celebrating the change of season and for happy occasions. Typically sushi rice is mixed with various ingredients, and then topped with seasonal vegetables, fish or egg. You can make chirashi-zushi with left-over ingredients. This is good for school lunches, but do not use raw fish.

Chirashi-zushi in cups
For a party, serve chirashi-zushi in a small cup with a spoon and add your choice of ingredients.

Chirashi-zushi

Serves 4

2–4 dried shiitake mushrooms
2 cups (18 fl oz/500 ml) water
1 tablespoon soy sauce
1 tablespoon superfine (caster) sugar or
  raw sugar
2 tablespoons fresh or frozen green peas
  or snow peas (mange tout), precooked
4 flower-shaped carrot slices (see
  Garnishes and Decorations)
4 cooked jumbo shrimp (king prawns)
1 egg

½ teaspoon superfine (caster) or raw sugar
pinch of salt
drop of vegetable oil
14 oz (400 g) sushi rice
1 tablespoon denbu (lightly mashed fish)
4 slices kamaboko fish cake
soy sauce, to serve
Cooked English spinach, lotus root, okra,
  broccoli, grilled eel (unagi), beni-shoga
  (pickled red ginger), avocado, smoked
  salmon (optional)

Soak the mushrooms in the water in a saucepan until soft, about 30 minutes. Once softened, remove from the saucepan and trim off the stems. Return the mushrooms to the water. Add the soy sauce and sugar. Bring to the boil, turn the heat to low and cook for 20 minutes. Remove from the heat and leave until cool.

With your hands, lightly squeeze the liquid from the shiitake mushrooms and place on a chopping board, then slice with a knife.

Cook the carrots in boiling water for 3 minutes and drain.

To prepare the shrimp, remove the heads and shells without cutting off the tail. Remove the vein.

Crack the eggs into a bowl and beat with the sugar and salt until dissolved.

In a non-stick frying pan, heat a few drops of oil, then cook the egg over a low heat, until it scrambles. Set aside.

If using frozen kamaboko, cook first in boiling water.

Place sushi rice in a bowl, mix in the denbu and scatter the mushrooms, carrots, shrimp, scrambled egg, kamaboko fish cake on top. Serve with soy sauce.

CHIRASHI-ZUSHI WITH NANOHANA

Serves 4

1 bunch of nanohana (canola or rape-flower) stems, cleaned and washed (see note)
pinch of salt
1 cup (8 fl oz/250 ml) bonito stock, cooled
1 tablespoon Japanese or English mustard
2 teaspoons light-coloured soy sauce
1 tablespoon mirin
4 bowls of cooked sushi rice
⅓ cup (75 ml/2½ fl oz) salmon caviar

Trim the nanohana and blanch with a pinch of salt. Drain then soak in iced water until cool. Drain again and squeeze out the excess water with your hands. Cut into 5 cm (2 in)-long pieces.

Soak the nanohana in bonito stock for about 1 hour.

Combine the mustard, soy sauce and mirin.

Take the nanohana out of the stock and place on kitchen paper to drain the excess liquid. Add the nanohana to the mustard sauce and combine.

Place the mixture on top of the sushi rice and top with salmon caviar.

NOTE: To enhance presentation, I would choose nanohana with yellow flowers

Seafood chirashi-zushi

Serves 4

1 lb 6 oz (600 g) sushi rice
1¾ oz (50 g) lotus roots, plus 1 teaspoon
  rice vinegar and 2 cups (18 fl oz/500 ml)
  water for soaking
2 tablespoons rice vinegar
1 teaspoon superfine (caster) sugar
pinch of salt

3½ oz (100 g) tuna or salmon (sashimi
  quality)
1½ oz (40 g) salmon caviar
1 Japanese thick omelette (see Preparing
  Fillings for Nori Rolls)
a few beansprouts

Peel the lotus root then slice thinly. Soak in the water for 5 minutes.

Meanwhile mix the rice vinegar with the sugar and a pinch of salt in a plastic container.

Bring a saucepan of water to the boil.

Take the lotus root out of the vinegar water, place it in the boiling water, cook for 2 minutes, then drain. Transfer the lotus root into the vinegar mixture and leave for 30 minutes. Strain before adding to rice.

With a knife slice the tuna into ⅔ in (1.5 cm) thick slices.

Slice the omelette into ⅔ in (1.5 cm) strips.

Place rice in individual small bowls.

Arrange the tuna, salmon caviar, lotus roots, omelette and bean sprouts on top.
Serve with soy sauce

Salmon can be used instead of tuna. Other possible ingredients include jumbo shrimp (king prawns) or cucumber.
You can colour the lotus pink by adding food colouring or natural colouring, such as beetroot juice to the vinegar mixture, if you like.

NEW-STYLE CHIRASHI-ZUSHI

Serves 4

4 cherry tomatoes
½ pink grapefruit or a handful of blueberries
4 chicory or salad leaves
2 anchovies (or salami, if you prefer)
14 oz (600 g) sushi rice
4 strips of red capsicum (bell pepper), diced
4 walnuts
Parmesan cheese, shaved (grated)
1 teaspoon Soy Sauce Jelly (see recipe)

With a small knife, cut the cherry tomatoes in half.

Peel the grapefruit and separate the segments. Discard the skin and cut each segment into 3 pieces.

Tear the chicory into bite-sized pieces.

Chop the anchovies or salami.

Add the sushi rice and all of the ingredients in a serving bowl and toss with a wooden spoon. Divide the rice between the 4 salad leaves.

Scatter the Parmesan over the sushi and decorate with soy sauce jelly.

Temaki-zushi

Temaki-zushi

Temaki-zushi, hand-wrapped sushi cones, are made of a hand-rolled sheet of nori filled with sushi rice and a variety of other ingredients. It is the easiest type of sushi to make at home. You can also use other wrap ingredients, such as omelettes, rice paper or salad leaves.

Temaki-zushi is suitable for a special lunch/dinner or a casual party for people who enjoy making sushi to their own taste. The method is simple; you just need to prepare sushi rice and the fillings, then set the table. Prepare the fillings ahead of time and arrange them attractively in separate bowls or on one large platter, on the table. Also it doesn't take much time to adjust the amount of the ingredients.

If you're hosting a temaki-zushi party, give your guests a little guidance on how to make the cone and then let them try it for themselves.

Sample Guidance Note:

Pick a sheet of nori and spoon sushi rice on the centre, slightly flatten and spread. Choose fillings and arrange on the rice along with your choice of sauce or paste. Then wrap up.

TEMAKI-ZUSHI

serves 1 (makes 4 slices)

For temaki-zushi, a half or quarter-sized nori sheet is used.

4–6 whole nori sheets, halved or quartered
sauces and dressings, such as soy sauce or mayonnaise, (see Dressings in Basic
   Techniques)
3–4 cups (21–28 oz/585–780 g) sushi rice, in a large bowl with a scoop
3 fillings of your choice

To make quarter-sized nori, fold in half and then quarters. Press the fold lines and cut along them to make square sheets.

How to prepare ingredients:
Choose a variety of fillings (see Preparing fillings for nori rolls).
- Vegetables: carrot, watercress, cucumber, green salad, avocado,
- Meat: chicken, jumbo shrimp (king prawn), crab meat stick, omelette, grilled (broiled) eel, ham, salmon (smoked, tinned or fresh), tuna (fresh or tinned)

How to roll temaki with a half-sized nori sheet:
- In your left hand hold a sheet of nori horizontally and with a wet spoon put sushi rice in the centre and slightly spread it over the nori sheet in a line across one corner (see photos 1, 2 and 3).
- Add a little mayonnaise to taste. Place any combination of the fillings on top (see photo 4).
- With your right hand wrap up the nori, making a cone shape (see photo 5 and 6).
- Spoon caviar on top if you like.
- Serve with soy sauce.

Temaki-zushi in crêpe

makes 12

1 cup (4 oz/115 g) all-purpose (plain) flour
1 cup (250 ml/8 fl oz) water
1 egg
vegetable oil, for cooking
1 tablespoon mayonnaise
2 tablespoons sushi rice
1 crab stick, halved
2 avocado slices
2 small salad leaves

In a bowl, add the flour, water and egg. Mix with chopsticks or a fork. Strain through a strainer into a bowl. Set aside to rest for 30 minutes.

Heat a non-stick frying pan over low heat and add some vegetable oil. When the pan is hot, ladle one-sixth of the batter mixture into the pan, moving the pan around so that it covers the base of the pan. When the surface begins to set, gently insert the spatula under the edge and turn over to cook the other side. Remove and set aside to cool.

Repeat to make a total of 6 crêpes. Cut each in half.

Spread mayonnaise on the centre of each crêpe.

Arrange salad leaf, rice and half a crab stick and avocado on each crêpe. Roll them up, making cone shapes.

Other sushi

OSHI-ZUSHI OR HAKO-ZUSHI

Oshi-zushi (pressed sushi) or hako-zushi (box sushi) is sushi rice that has been pressed into a box mould, with other ingredients as a topping. The mould is removed and layers are cut into bite-sized pieces. The sushi mould consists of a box with two lids. But it is only available from a specialised Japanese shop.
Here we use a small cake tin (pan) about 5½ x 2¾ in (14 x 7 cm).

makes 1 box

1–1¾ oz (30–50 g) smoked salmon*
3–3½ oz (90–100 g) sushi rice
1 tablespoon ricotta cheese
mustard cress or green salad leaves, to decorate

Arrange plastic wrap around the base and sides of the tin.
   Arrange smoked salmon slices on the base. Fill with sushi rice to the top of the tin.
   If you have another tin of the same size, use the bottom of the empty tin to press firmly on the top of the full tin; or use a spoon to set evenly.
   Carefully turn it over onto a dry chopping board.
   With moistened knife, slice into 6 pieces and arrange on a plate.
   Decorate with ricotta cheese and mustered cress on top.

You may use grilled eel instead of smoked salmon.

Moulded/cup sushi

This is an easy and colourful sushi. Just mix sushi rice with other ingredients and mould with a small cup or cookie cutter.

BROCCOLI CUP SUSHI

makes 2 cups

1¾ oz (50 g) broccoli
½ teaspoon olive oil
5–6 oz (140–175 g) sushi rice or pink rice
soy sauce, to serve

Divide the broccoli into small pieces. Cook in boiling water for 1 minute and strain. Refresh under running water and drain well. Keep two pieces for decoration and chop the others with a knife on a chopping board.

Place the chopped broccoli in a small bowl and mix with olive oil.

With a moistened rice spatula, combine the sushi rice with chopped broccoli.

Slightly wet one cup and using a rice spatula, stuff with sushi rice. With the other empty cup, press to firm the rice.

Turn the sushi upside down on a serving plate and remove from the cup by tapping the base with your hand.

Top with a piece of broccoli as a decoration.

TOBIKO-CUP SUSHI

makes 2 cups

5 oz (150 g) sushi rice
2 teaspoons tobiko (flying fish roe)
2 teaspoons cottage cheese

soy sauce, to serve
few sprigs fennel

Place sushi rice and tobiko in a bowl and combine with a moistened rice spatula.

Slightly wet a cup and stuff with sushi rice using a rice spatula. With the base of another empty cup, press to firm.

Turn the sushi upside down on a serving plate and remove from the cup by tapping the base with your hand.

Top with cottage cheese and garnish with sprigs of fennel.

TUNA AND CUCUMBER CUP SUSHI

makes 2 cups

5 oz (150 g) sushi rice
$^2/_3$ oz (20 g) canned tuna
¾ oz (20 g) Lebanese cucumber, chopped
2 teaspoons mayonnaise

carrot flower and cottage cheese, for
   decoration
soy sauce, to serve

Place the sushi rice, tuna and cucumber in a bowl and combine with a moistened rice spatula.

Slightly wet one cup and stuff with sushi rice using a rice spatula. With another empty cup press to firm.

Turn the sushi out on a serving plate and remove from the cup by tapping the base with your hand. Top with carrot flower petal and cottage cheese.

Corn cup sushi

makes 2 cups

1¾ oz (50 g) sweetcorn cobs
¼ teaspoon butter
5 oz (150 g) sushi rice
carrot bands, to garnish
slices of lime, to garnish
wasabi tobiko, to garnish
soy sauce, to serve

Cook the corn in boiling water. Remove from the pan, cut off kernels with a knife and mix with butter while still warm.

Add the sushi rice to the corn and mix to combine with a moistened rice spatula.

Slightly wet a cup and stuff with sushi rice. With another empty cup press to firm.

Turn the sushi upside down on a serving plate and remove from the cup by tapping the base with your hand.

Serve Corn cup sushi with a carrot band, topped with a slice of lime and wasabi tobiko.

Tulip-shaped sushi with pink denbu flakes

makes 1 small tulip-shaped sushi

¼–½ cup sushi rice (the amount you need depends on the size of the cutter)
1 teaspoon denbu (fish and sugar, see Japanese groceries)
1 mint leaves, with a stalk

Dampen a cutter in a bowl of water. Transfer it onto the plate. Use it as a mould and stuff with sushi rice using a moistened spatula or spoon.

Spread denbu over the top.

Carefully remove the cutter from the formed rice.

Arrange mint leaves as the stem of the flower.

Choose pink sushi rice/coloured sushi rice instead of denbu, if you like.

Fukusa-zushi (wrapped sushi in omelette)

makes 4

5½ oz (160 g) sushi rice
1 tablespoon canned tuna or 1 teaspoon chopped anchovies
½ teaspoon soy sauce
½ teaspoon white roasted sesame seeds
option: you may mix rice with grated (shredded) or chopped fresh ginger, green peas,
   etc.
4 blanched chives or mitsuba
4 thin omelettes (see Preparing Fillings for Nori Rolls)

Using a moistened spoon, mix the sushi rice with tuna, soy sauce and sesame seeds in
a bowl.

   Arrange the omelette on a dry plate and spoon the rice on the centre. Wrap the rice
in the omelette, folding in the corners like a parcel. Tie a chive around the centre.

Index

About the Author

Hideo Dekura was born in Tokyo and started his training in his family's two restaurants. Here he learnt the principles of sushi and kappou-ryori food preparation, cooking and presentation. At the same time he studied the philosophy of Chakaiseki (the cuisine of the tea ceremony), Teikanryu Shodo (calligraphy), Ikenobo-Ryûseiha (flower arrangement) and Hocho Shiki (the ceremony of the cooking knife) from Iemoto-Shishikura Soken-sensei under the authority of Shijyoshinryû.

In 2007, the Japanese government presented Hideo with an award for making a significant contribution to the promotion of Japanese food and cooking.

Hideo runs the Japanese cooking studio, Culinary Studio Dekura, works as a food consultant and is known as an expert in all aspects of Japanese cuisine.